Samsung Galaxy S4 Ma

The Beginner's Samsung Galaxy S4 User Guide

Master your powerful new device with this Samsung Galaxy S4 Manual for Beginners. This smartphone is powerful, yet daunting and complicated. Don't get left in the dust! Francis Monico's guide will help you tap all of the device's advanced features like a seasoned pro.

By Francis Monico

Table of Contents

Choosing Your Galaxy: S3 vs. S4

For those with the Samsung Galaxy S3 that are still wondering if it's time to make the switch, this guidebook will first cover the differences between the two and then dive into the features of the Samsung Galaxy S4.

Screen

The S3's screen is only 4.8-inches while the new phone stretches to a 5-inch screen. The SuperAMOLED technology can be found within both devices. Even the resolution has increased from 720x1280 to 1080x1920, for a clearer image and more pixel density—moving from 306ppi to 441ppi.

Camera

In 2012, the S3's 8MP camera was pretty standard for the time period. The S4 comes with a 13Mp rear camera and a 2.1Mp front camera for higher image quality and video chatting. The video records in Full HD 1080p, while the S3 records at 720p.

Design

While the design is similar, the main difference is that the S4 is larger. Slightly more squared than rounded, the new edition resembles the S2. The home button is in the same location but is a difference shape; the rear cover is basically the same as well.

Despite having a larger screen, the actual body of the S4 is actually smaller than the S3. The height still stands firm at 136.6mm but the newer model is slightly smaller, coming in at 69.8mm, rather than

70.6mm in width. The S3 also weighs slightly more weighing 133g, compared to the sleek new 130g of the S4.

Processor

The Samsung Galaxy S4 comes with the Exynos 5 Octa processor, where the previous phone used the Exynos 4 Quad processor. The S4 is the first smartphone to use an 8-core chip. The device features Cortex-A15 cores that register at 1.6Hz to help save power. The ram has also moved up from 1GB to 2GB (the UK model, however, will feature a 1.9GHz quad-core processor rather than the octa-core chip).

Software

For those who have been keeping up with the updates, the S3 should be running Android 4.1.2 Jelly Bean—the most up-to-date version. The S4 comes standard with the Android 4.2.2, along with TouchWiz user interface. The S4 also features Smart Scroll, Smart Pause, and Air Gesture.

Battery

The newer version should last longer than the older edition. The S4 features a 2600mAh battery while the S3 only comes with a 2100mAh battery. Both are removable and the only reason the S3 may last longer is because of all of the advances within the S4: larger screen, higher resolution, etc. The main difference should fall within the Exynos 5 processor that specifically works to help the device save power.

New Features

The following features are new to the Galaxy S4 or have had major upgrades. Use this as a reference to these new features available.

Camera

The Galaxy S4's camera has some major upgrades over the S3. These include Dual Camera mode, Sound & Shot mode, Drama Shot mode, and Eraser mode.

- Dual Camera Mode: In this mode you can take a picture of you, using the front camera and insert it into a video or picture that you are taking. To access this mode tap the Camera button > Auto > Dual Camera button (top left corner of screen) > Line up the camera and make sure your face is in the picture > tap the Arrow at the bottom of the screen to choose from 12 possible frames > Press the Shutter button.

- Sound & Shot Mode: This new feature allows you to listen to your photos! It allows you to record up to nine seconds audio with each still image. You record it after you've taken the photo and you must change the camera from Auto Shot to Sound & Shot modes after opening up the camera. Remember, if you download or copy the picture to your computer it will only be the image.

- Drama Shot Mode: Sometimes more than one click is needed to tell what is happening. In Drama shot you can create a collage of pictures simply by choosing Drama Shot when you enter into Camera mode. Drama Shot mode takes your pictures and then puts them into a single picture to create a better representation of what has happened.

- Eraser: In this mode you can erase moving objects from the background of a picture. You MUST change the camera mode to Eraser before taking the picture or you will not be able to use Eraser mode. Once you've taken the picture you can edit the picture, show or hide moving objects, and share with other S4 devices. If you export the picture to any non-

S4 device it will be a still picture with the original objects in it. When using this mode keep the following in mind:

- Keep the camera steady
- Try avoiding the subject and background being the same color or too similar
- If the subject is moving too much or too little it may not work
- If there are multiple subjects moving too much in the background the camera may not pick up on each of them.

S Translator

Using this feature allows you to say or text directly into your S4 and it will read or text back the translation for you! Right now there are nine languages available for translation: Chinese, French, German, Italian, Japanese, Korean, Portuguese, Spanish, and English. You do need a data connection for this to work.

Home Sync

This is a personal cloud device used for family entertainment and has a 1TB capacity for storage. You can use it to bring games, movies, and TV Shows onto your TV using the service. It also includes Mirror Mouse as a specialized navigational feature to use all the features available in HomeSync. Since it's a cloud storage device it is easy to upload and sync it with other devices you may have.

S Voice

This feature allows for voice activated commands. This allows you to make phone calls, search on the internet, use the navigation, send text messages, or even speak into the Memo option and creates note for yourself.

ChatOn

Want to show someone what is on your screen? With ChatOn you can show up two others what you can see on your own screen. You can even give them access to what's on your phone and create masks to create a frame around them or change the background to enhance the experience even more. You can access this feature while you are in a chat by using the menu button.

Air Gesture / Air Viewer

Using this feature allows you to wave your hand over the Galaxy S4 to accept calls, browse the web, look at pictures, or even change the music that is playing. With Air View you are able to enlarge photos, take a sneak peak at emails and use your speed dial settings while slightly placing your finger over the intended area. This can all be done even while wearing gloves.

Samsung Smart Scroll

This new feature allows you to scroll through pages in your phone with a slight screen tilt and a look of your eyes moving up or down. To access this feature and enable it simply: Select Apps > Settings > Navigate to My Device > Hit Smart screen > Turn on Smart scroll.

Smart Pause

Once this feature is enabled it will automatically stop playing a video once you look away. To enable it: Open the Settings menu > My Device > Smart Screen > Check Smart pause.

S Health

Now you can use your S4 to stay active and fit. This feature will track workouts, weight, and you can even input what you eat and drink. It will even tell you the current temperature and humidity so you know how comfortable you will be while working out. The Health Board will show you different charts to help you visualize your progress. Some accessories may need additional updates as well as 3rd party apps depending on the country and service provider.

WatchON

This feature turns your S4 into a smart remote for your TV. It will even suggest various programs based on your watching preferences. It will also connect to your home entertainment system, channel surf for you, and schedule programs to watch.

Learning the Basics

Layout & Buttons

Layout:

Front view:

<u>Top left</u>
Light sensor
Notification light

<u>Top center</u>
Earpiece

<u>Top right</u>
Proximity/Gesture sensor
Front camera

<u>Right hand side</u>
Power button
The front panel is dedicated to the touch screen

<u>Bottom left</u>
Menu button

<u>Bottom center</u>
Home button

<u>Bottom right</u>
Back button

Around the edges:

<u>Top right</u>
IR (Infrared) LED

<u>Top left</u>

Microphone for speakerphone and Headset jack

Left hand side
Volume button

Bottom left
Microphone

Bottom right
Multipurpose jack

Rear view:

Top left
GPS antenna

Top center
Rear camera and flash
The rear panel is dominated by the back cover

Bottom left
Speaker

The main antenna is in the bottom quarter of the phone
The microphone is active only when the speakerphone or video camera is in use.
Covering the antenna with your hands or other objects may drain the battery or cause you to lose connectivity.
Screen protectors may interfere with the sensor.
Keep the touch screen dry.
Liquids and humidity may cause your phone to malfunction.

Buttons:

Power button
To switch the device on or off, press and hold. If the phone has fatal errors/hang-ups or freezes, press and hold for 7 seconds to reset. This button is also used to lock or unlock the device, which also goes into lock mode when the touch screen turns off.

Menu button
To open a list of options available for the current screen, tap the menu button.To launch Google search, tap and hold the menu button on the main screen.

Home button
Pressing this button will return to the Home screen. For a list of recent applications, press and hold the Home button.

Back button
Tapping this button will return you to the previous screen.

Volume button
Used for adjusting the device volume.

SIM Card & Battery

Installation of SIM card and battery

Insert the SIM or USIM card and battery.
- Only microSIM cards will fit.
- Refer to your Service Provider for LTE service availability.

Remove back cover, taking care not to damage your fingernails. Bending or twisting the back cover too much could damage it. Next ensure that the gold-colored contacts are facing down and insert the SIM or USIM card, then slide the SIM or USIM card into the correct slot until it lock in place. (Take care not to insert a memory card into the SIM card slot. Should this happen, take the device to a Service Center for removal.) Finally, push the battery into place and attach the back cover.

Removal of SIM card and battery

Take the back cover off and remove the battery. Before pulling the SIM or USIM card out, push it to disengage it from the slot.

Battery Charging

Before using the device for the first time, the battery needs to be charged. This can be done with a charger or by connecting the device to a computer with a USB cable. If the battery is running low, a warning tone will sound and a low battery power message will be appear on the screen

If the battery is completely flat, the phone will not turn on immediately when attached to the charger. Allow the battery to charge for a while before trying to switch the phone on.

If you intend using multiple applications, network applications or applications which interact with other devices, you are advised to only do so after fully charging the battery to avoid losing network connectivity due to your battery running flat.

Using the Charger

The end of the USB cable must get plugged into the multipurpose jack after the USB cable has been connected to the USB power adaptor. The device may be damaged if connected incorrectly

Using the device while charging may lengthen the amount of time taken for charging.
If the touch screen stops responding while charging, unplug the device from the charger. This may happen if the power supply is erratic.

It is normal for the device to get hot during charging, but it will stop charging if it gets too hot

Once the battery is fully charged, disconnect the charger from the phone before unplugging the charger from the power source. Removing the battery before the charger may damage your phone. The charger should be unplugged when not in use to conserve energy, since it does not have its own power switch

The battery status icons will indicate whether the battery is charging or fully charged. To reduce the amount of power used, certain features can be deactivated and or customized.

Try the following power saving tips:

- If you are not actively using the device, activate sleep mode with the Power button.
- Use the task manager to deactivate applications, which are not being used.
- Reduce backlight time and display brightness.
- Switch off WiFi, Bluetooth and automatic synchronizing.

Memory Card

While some memory cards may not be compatible with your device, you should be able to use most memory cards with a maximum of 64G capacity. Using a card that is not designed to work with your phone may cause damage to the card or corruption of data. Always take care to insert the memory card right-side up.

FAT and exFAT file systems are supported and your phone will prompt you to reformat any memory card that is formatted differently.

Your memory card will have a shorter lifespan if you frequently write and erase data.
You will find your memory card in the SD memory card folder of the phone's internal memory after insertion.

Memory Card Insertion

After removing the back cover, ensure that the gold-colored contacts are facing downwards before pushing the card into the slot and locking it in place. Finally put the back cover on again.

Memory Card Removal

The memory card must be unmounted before removal by tapping the following sequence on the Home screen: Apps > Settings > More > Storage > Unmount SD Card.

After removing the back cover, push the memory card to disengage and pull it out. Finally put the back cover on again.

Removing the memory card while it is in use may cause data corruption and damage to the card and phone.

Memory Card Formatting

Please format you card on your phone, since a memory card formatted on a computer may be incompatible with your phone. Remember to backup any data you want to keep before formatting your memory card.

The memory card is formatted by tapping the following sequence on the Home screen: Apps > Settings > More > Storage > Format SD card > Format SD card > Erase everything

Volume

To adjust ringtone, music or video volume, press the Volume button on the side of the phone up or down.

Silent Mode

There are 3 ways to activate Silent mode:

1. Press Volume button and hold until Silent mode is activated.
2. Tap Mute or Vibrate while holding the power button.
3. Tap Sound or Vibrate after opening the notifications panel (top of screen).

Touch Screen

- Your touch screen is designed for fingers only.

- Keep other electrical devices away from the touch screen.

- Keep the touch screen dry. Liquids and humidity may cause your phone to malfunction.

- Do not use sharp objects on your touch screen. Also avoid pressing too hard with your fingers.

- It is advisable to switch off the touch screen when your phone is not in use to avoid after-images.

- Opening applications, selecting menu items, onscreen buttons and keyboard usage are all actions performed by tapping the touch screen with your finger.

- Available options are accessed by tapping and holding for more than 2 seconds.

- Tapping and holding an item while dragging it, will move said item to a new location.

- You zoom in and out of images, maps and web pages by double tapping.

- To see another panel, flick left or right on the Home screen. To scroll, flick up or down.

- To zoom in on part of a web page, map or image, spread 2 fingers apart, or pinch them together.

Indicator Signals

Various icons/indicator signals are displayed at the top and bottom of the screen, to show the current status of your phone. Some of these indicators are:

Air gesture active
Alarm active
Battery power level
Bluetooth active
Call in progress
Connected to computer
EDGE connection
Error occurred or caution required
Flight mode active
GPRS connection
GPS active
HSDPA connection
HSPA+ connection
LTE connection
Missed call
New text or multimedia message
No signal
No SIM or USIM card
Roaming (outside of normal service area)
Signal strength
Silent mode active
Smart scroll feature active
Synced with the web
UMTS connection
Vibration mode active
WiFi connection

Palm Controls

Palm controls are activated from the Home screen as follows: tap Apps > Settings > My device > Motions and gestures > Palm motion and drag the Palm motions switch to the right.

To capture a screen shot, sweep your hand across the screen.

To pause media playback, cover the screen with your palm.

Air View/Air Gesture

Activate these features as follows:

- Tap Apps > Settings > My device > Motions and gestures > Air gesture and drag the Air gesture switch to the right.
- Tap Apps > Settings > My device > Air view and drag the Air view switch to the right.

Do not cover your hand with anything dark or the phone may not pick up the movements made.

- Moving your hand above the sensor when the screen is switched off will allow you to view various notifications, such as missed calls, new messages, etc.
- Moving your hand up and down in front of the sensor will allow you to scroll up and down.
- To browse images, web content, songs or memos, move your hand left or right in front of the sensor.
- To move an icon to another location, tap and hold the icon with one hand, while moving your other hand left or right in front of the sensor.
- To answer an incoming call, move your hand left, then right, in front of the sensor.
- Air view allows you to view content or information in a popup window by pointing at an item with your finger.

Smart Pause

Smart pause enables you to pause video when you look away from the screen & restart when you look back again. Activate by tapping Apps > Settings > My device > Smart screen and selecting Smart pause.

Smart Control

Smart control allows you to scroll up and down while viewing emails by merely moving your head. It is activated by tapping Apps > Settings > My device > Smart screen > Smart scroll and then dragging the Smart scroll switch to the right.

Notifications

At the top of the screen, on the status bar, you will find various icons notifying you of the following events: missed calls, calendar events, phone status, etc.

To see the notifications panel, drag it down from the status bar (drag up from the bottom of the screen to close). Once the notifications panel is open, you can scroll to see additional alerts

Glove Mode

Glove mode enables you to use the touch screen with gloves on. Leather gloves are preferred to other materials. The screen should be tapped firmly when wearing gloves.
Due to the heightened sensitivity of the touch screen in this mode, accidental inputs may occur once gloves have been removed.

This mode is activated from the Home screen as follows: tap Apps > Settings > My device > Display. After, select High touch sensitivity.

Multi-Window

This feature enables split screen processing and is enabled from the Home screen as follows: tap Apps > Settings > My device > Display, thereafter select Multi-window

- This feature is region and service provider dependent

- When running multimedia files such as video or music, sound will

be played from both applications.

- You can only run applications found on the Multi-window panel.

- Activation of the Multi-window panel is achieved by tapping and holding the Back button. The panel will appear on the left side of the screen. Select an application & drag another to a new location. Tapping and holding the Back button again will hide the panel. The size of the windows can be adjusted by dragging the bar between the applications up and down. The window can be moved around by tapping and dragging the handle towards the left or right side of the screen.
- Other options available for Multi-window are accessed using the up and down arrow icons. Tapping them will activate icons enabling you to switch between applications, close applications and maximize applications.

Settings Panel

The Settings panel enables you to view the settings currently active on your phone.
Access the Settings panel by dragging the status bar down and tapping the Settings panel icon. This gives access to the following options:

Activation and deactivation of WiFi and WiFi hotspot detection
Activation and deactivation of GPS
Activation and deactivation of Silent mode, including mute and vibrate options
Screen rotation settings
Activation and deactivation of Bluetooth
Activation and deactivation of Blocking mode. Selection of notifications to be blocked and unblocked are made by tapping Settings > My device > Blocking mode
Activation and deactivation of Mobile data connection
Activation and deactivation of power-saving mode
Activation and deactivation of Screen mirroring
Multi window
Activation and deactivation of S Beam
Activation and deactivation of NFC

Activation and deactivation of Air view
Activation and deactivation of Air gesture
Activation and deactivation of Driving mode
Activation and deactivation of Smart stay
Activation and deactivation of Smart scroll
Activation and deactivation of automatic synchronizing
Activation and deactivation of Flight mode

Some of the above options are region and service provider
dependent.
The notifications panel can be rearranged by tapping the Settings
panel icon and then the edit icon. You then select the icon you want
moved and drag it to a new position.

Home Screen

- The Home screen gives you access to all of your phone's features.

- The Home screen's multiple panels may be viewed by scrolling left

or right

- The Home screen has 2 modes, namely basic and easy. Shortcuts

can be added to the - = - Home screen in easy mode which is

accessed as follows: tap Apps > Settings > My device > Home

screen mode > Easy mode > Apply.

- To add an icon to the Home screen, tap Apps and tap and hold the

application you want to add and drag it into a preview panel.

- Widgets, folders and pages can also be added to the Home screen

as follows: tap and hold the home screen's empty area and select

the option which coincides with the item you want to add to the

Home screen

- Items can be moved by tapping, holding and then dragging them

to the desired location. - Dragging an item to the side of the screen

will move it to a new panel

24

- To remove an item, tap and drag to the Trash bin at the top of the

Home screen. Release when the trash bin turns red

The following options are available for panels:

Add: tap Menu > edit page > +
Move: tap Menu > edit page > tap and hold the panel and drag it
into its new position.
Delete: tap Menu > edit page > tap and hold panel, dragging it to the
trash bin at the top of the screen.

Images and photos stored on the phone can be set as wallpaper as
follows:
Tap Menu > Set wallpaper > Home screen

- You can now choose Gallery (photos and downloaded images),

Live wallpapers or Wallpapers. Next choose your wallpaper and tap

Set wallpaper. Alternatively, choose a picture, drag the frame to

change its size and tap on Done.

- Widgets, which are mini-apps with specific functions, can be added

to the Home screen from the Widget panel. Some of these require

an internet connection and may add to your data costs. Some

widgets are region and service provider dependent.

- Widgets are added to the Home screen as follows: in the Home

screen tap Apps > Widgets. Scroll left or right to find your widget

and then select it to add it to the Home screen

A shortcut to a widget may be created on the Home screen by
tapping Apps > Widgets and then selecting Settings Shortcut, which
reveals a list of options. Choose an option to create the shortcut on
the Home screen

Bluetooth

- Bluetooth can be used to wirelessly connect 2 devices that are close to each other for the purposes of exchanging data.
- It is important to ensure that you connect to trusted and secured devices.
- If there are any objects (such as walls, furniture, etc) between the devices connected via Bluetooth, it may be necessary to bring them closer to one another.
- Your phone may be incompatible with certain other Bluetooth devices, such as those not yet tested by the Bluetooth Special Interest Group (Bluetooth SIG).
- Bluetooth should not be used for piracy, illegally intercepting communications, or any other illegal activities.
- Bluetooth is activated via the Applications screen by tapping Settings > Connections > Bluetooth, then dragging the switch to the right.
- To pair your phone to another Bluetooth device via the Applications screen, tap Settings > Connections > Bluetooth > Scan. Bluetooth devices in your vicinity will be displayed and you can select the one you wish to pair with. An automatically generated key will be displayed on both devices. Accept the key to complete the pairing.
- Sending data from within a Bluetooth enabled application is done as follows: Open the app, select the item you wish to send, tap Bluetooth, select a discovered device and accept the request from the other device. Most files are saved to the Bluetooth folder, with

the exception of contacts, which are automatically added to the contact list.

Screen Mirroring

- Screen Mirroring enables you to share content on a large screen. Screen Mirroring is enabled via an AllShare Cast dongle, HomeSync or a device supporting WiFi Miracast.
- Screen Mirroring is region and service provider dependent. High-bandwidth Digital Content Protection, or HDCP, support may be required for Miracast enabled devices to work.
- This feature should be disabled when not in use to conserve energy.
- AllShare cast dongles and HomeSync may not be discovered if a frequency is specified
- When connection to a television, ensure that the correct television mode has been selected
- Activation of Screen Mirroring via the Applications screen is as follows: tap Settings > Connections > Screen Mirroring > drag switch to the right. Once a device has been chosen and a file or application has been chosen, adjust the display from your phone. If you wish to use a PIN, tap and hold the chosen device to enter the PIN.

Communications

Contacts

- Phone numbers, email addresses and other information is managed via the Contacts application which is accessed by tapping Contacts on the Applications screen.
- Contacts are created by tapping the Add Contact icon
- Images may be assigned to contacts using the Avatar icon
- Fields can be added to or removed from a contact using the + or − icons.
- Contacts are edited by selecting a contact and using the edit icon.
- To delete a contact, select the contact, tap Menu > Delete.
- To set up speed dial for a contact, tap Menu > Speed Dial Setting. Select a number and select the contact you wish to assign to that speed dial number. A speed dial is removed by tapping and holding the speed dial number and tapping Remove.
- You can search for contacts by scrolling through your contacts lists, entering search criteria in the search field above your contacts or using the index to the right of the contacts list by dragging.
- Once a contact has been selected, you can add to Favorites, initiate voice or video calls Call > create Messages or create Emails.
- All contacts saved on the phone, SIM card, USIM card or another account are displayed by default. To change the source for displayed contacts tap Menu > and select the source you want to use.

Contacts can be moved (or merged) as follows:

-Move to Google: tap Menu > Merge Accounts > Merge with Google (these contacts will be assigned the Google icon).

-Move to Samsung: tap Menu > Merge Accounts > Merge with contacts (these contacts will be assigned the Samsung icon).

To import or export contacts, tap Menu > Import/Export > select the option for importing or exporting contacts to or from your chosen source (SIM card, SD card, USB).

Contacts can be shared by tapping Menu > Import/Export > Share name-card via >select the desired contacts > done > select method (Bluetooth, email, etc).

Contacts can be managed by tapping Menu and selecting the desired option such as search; add to favorites; remove from favorites; grid view/list view or help.

Add a contact to an existing group by selecting the group and tapping the Add Contact icon. Select the contact(s) you wish to add and tap done.

- Contact groups can be managed by tapping Menu and selecting the desired option such as create; search; change order; delete groups or help.

- Messages may be sent to group members by tapping Menu > Send message/email > select members > done.

- To create and share your own business card as follows: tap set up my profile > enter desired details > tap save > tap Menu> share name-card via > select method (Bluetooth, email, etc).

Phone & Messaging

Phone application

- The phone application is used to make outgoing and answer incoming calls.
- Access the application by tapping Phone on the Applications screen.
- Outgoing calls are initiated via the keypad (enter the number and tap the call icon); from your call logs; from your favorites menu; from your contacts list or by tapping and holding the chosen digit on your speed dial list.
- When using the keypad to enter a number, your phone will automatically try to predict the number you are calling. Select the desired number or contact if it appears onscreen.

- To place an international call, tap and hold 0 until it changes to a + sign; enter country code, area code and telephone number and then tap the call icon.
- Some additional options are available while a call is in progress, such as: equalizer options; noise reduction; increase or decrease volume; hold; add call; keypad; end call; speaker; mute; headset; swap; merge; open contacts; create memo; send   message; transfer call; manage conference call.
- Contacts are added by entering a number and tapping add to contacts.
- Call logs are accessed by tapping Logs. To view only specific calls, tap Menu > view by > select viewing option.

- Your phone can be set to dial only numbers with specific prefixes. This is done by tapping Menu > call settings > additional settings > fixed dialing numbers > enable FDN > enter supplied PIN2 > tap FDN list > add numbers.

- To activate call barring tap Menu > call settings > additional settings > call barring > select call type and barring options and enter a password.

- Calls are answered by dragging the call icon out of the large circle, or by pressing the headset button. Another call can be made if call waiting is active, with the 1st call being placed on hold as soon as the 2nd call is answered.

- To reject a call, drag the end call button out of the large circle, or press and hold the headset button.

To set up and send a rejection message for calls tap Menu > call settings > set up call reject messages. Dragging the reject message bar up will send the rejection message when rejecting a call.

You can automatically reject calls from specified numbers by tapping Menu > call settings > call rejection > auto reject mode > auto reject numbers > auto reject list > create > enter a number, choose a category and save.

Missed calls are indicated on the status bar and can be accessed via the Notifications panel.
If your service provider supports call waiting, it can be set up as follows: tap Menu > call settings > additional settings > call waiting. This is not possible during video calls.

Incoming calls can be redirected to a different number by tapping Menu > call settings > additional settings > call forwarding > select pertinent options > enter the number you want the calls directed to > enable.

Calls are ended by tapping the call end icon, or holding the headset button

Video calls are initiated in the same manner as voice calls, except that the video call icon is tapped, rather than the call icon.

Some additional options which are available during video calls include switch camera; mute; end call; hide me; outgoing image; keypad; switch to headset; speaker off; animated emotions; theme view; enable cartoon view; dual camera; capture image; record video; switch camera; outgoing image; swap image.

Messaging Application

- This application is used to send text (SMS) messages or multimedia (MMS) messages and is accessed by tapping Messaging on the applications screen.
- To send a message tap the compose icon > add recipients by entering a number or tapping the contacts icon > type your message and tap the send icon.
- Images, events, video etc. can be added to the message (making it a multimedia message) by tapping the attachment icon.
- To add a subject to you MMS, tap Menu > Add subject.
- Messages can be scheduled to send on a specific date at a specific time by tapping
Menu > Scheduled message prior to sending the message.
- Scheduled messages will only send at the specified time if the phone is switched on and connected to a network.
- Messages can be translated by tapping Menu > translate > drag translate switch to right > select a language pair > OK during message composition. Tap the translation icon and done. - The original message will be replaced with a translation.
- Incoming messages can be read by selecting a contact and viewing the messages which they have sent to you.
- To listen to voicemail messages, tap and hold 1 on the keypad.

Talk

This application enables the use of Google Talk. Tap Talk on the applications screen for access. This service is region and service provider specific.

- To change your profile, select the account ID at the top of the screen. This will allow you to change your availability, avatar & status message.

- To add friends, tap the add friends icon > type in the email address > tap done.

- To chat to friends, select from friends list, enter a message at the bottom of the screen and tap the send message icon.

- Adding friends to chat is done by tapping Menu > add to chat.

- Ending a chat is done by tapping Menu > end chat.

- Switch between chats by scrolling left or right.

- Chat history is cleared by tapping Menu > clear chat history.

Email

Email is sent and received through the email application which is accessed by tapping email on the applications screen.

- Your initial email account is setup by entering the email address and password > tap next for private email, or manual setup for enterprise email > follow onscreen instructions.
- To set up additional email accounts tap Menu > settings > add account.
- To send messages, select the email address you wish to send from, then tap the compose icon (bottom of screen) enter recipients, a subject and type your message, then tap the send message icon.
- Additional recipients can be added using the contacts icon.
- Pictures and videos can be attached with the attachment icon, or embedded in the message by using the insert icon.

As with text messages, an email can be scheduled to be sent at a specific time on a specific date by tapping Menu > schedule sending > select schedule sending & specify your date and time for sending> tap done. The message will be sent at the appointed time if the phone is switched on and connected to a network.

When an email address is selected, new messages from that address are automatically retrieved. This can also be done manually by tapping the refresh icon. Tapping the message will open it for reading and make a few more options available, such as adding the sender to contacts; creating a reminder for the message; opening attachments; forwarding or deleting the message; replying to sender or all recipients. It is also possible to scroll between messages rather than closing each on and opening the next.

Google+

Tap Google+ on the applications screen to connect with people via Google's social networking application. This service is region and service provider dependent. Other social network features are available by tapping the Google icon.

Messenger

Messenger is used to chat to people via Google+ instant messaging and is accessed by tapping Messenger on the applications screen. To chat to friends, select from friends list, enter a message at the bottom of the screen and tap the send message icon.

Mass Media

Music

This application enables you to listen to music on your phone and is accessed by tapping on Music on the applications screen.

- To play music, select your category and song.

- Tapping the picture of the album at the bottom of your screen will bring up the music player screen, where the following options are made available:

-Play music on DLNA enabled devices
-Mark a song as favorite
-Turn the volume up and down
-Shuffle songs
-Repeat songs
-Hide the music player
-Open a playlist
-Pause and resume
-Restart a song
-Skip to previous song
-Rewind current song
-Skip to next song
-Fast forward through current song

Tap Menu > settings > smart volume to automatically adjust the volume for all songs.
You can set the song you are listening to as a ringtone by tapping Menu > set as > phone ringtone.

To create your own playlists tap playlists> Menu > create playlist > name your playlist > tap ok > tap add music > select songs > done.

The songs you are listening to can be added to a playlist by tapping Menu > add to playlist.

Your phone will automatically create a mood-based playlist. To add a piece of music to a particular mood, rather than the default, tap Music square> Menu > Library update. Select the cell with the desired mood, or drag multiple cells.

Camera and Gallery

The camera application is used to take photographs and video, which can be viewed in the Gallery. The camera application is accessed by tapping camera on the applications screen. The camera will be automatically switched off when not in use. Ensure that the camera lens is kept clean for use with high definition modes.

Taking Pictures

Tap the onscreen picture in the area where you would like to focus, when the camera is in focus, the focus frame will turn green. Tap the Camera to take the picture. Onscreen indicators and options are as follows: switch between front and rear camera; switch to dual camera mode; view more options; an indicator to show which mode is active; start taking video; select alternative shooting mode; view photos and video in gallery

Several photo effects or shooting modes are available:

Auto – the camera evaluates the environment and decides on the best mode

Beauty face – faces are lightened for gentler images

Best photo – a series of pictures are taken so that the best one may be saved

Best face – a series of multiple group shots are combined to create the best image

Sound and shot – take pictures with a few seconds of audio

Drama – used to take a series of pictures, which can be combined to show trails of movement

Animated photo – create animated pictures from video

Rich tone (HDR) – improved contrast ratio

Eraser – used to remove movements of objects in motion in the background

Panorama – one picture composed of many pictures strung together
Sports – used where the subject is moving quickly
Night – used for photos taken in low light conditions

Panoramic Photos

This is a series of pictures strung together to create a wide landscape image.

- Tap mode > panorama
- Tap Camera and move the camera (either left to right or right to left – do not go over the same area twice). Each time the blue frame lines up with the viewfinder, another picture is taken in the panoramic sequence.

Taking Videos

- Tap the Video icon to start recording, tap Pause to stop.
- While recording you can tap the camera icon to take a still shot and you can tap the screen to change the focus point.
- Possible recording modes are normal; limit for MMS; slow motion and fast motion.
- You can zoom in and out either with the volume control button, or by touching the screen with 2 fingers and pinching them together to zoom out and spreading them apart to zoom in.

- Dual camera mode, when taking landscape photos with the rear camera, the picture or video taken by the front camera (or the other way around) is shown as an insert.

- Share shot is used to send a picture directly from the camera to another device using either WiFi Direct or NFC.

- Buddy photo share allows your phone to recognize somebody you have tagged in previous pictures and send it to them.

- ChatON photo share sends pictures to other ChatON enabled devices.

Remote viewfinder allows a remote device to control the camera via WiFi Direct or NFC.

Camera Configuration Settings

The following camera configuration options are available, but some are dependent on the mode in use:

Photo size/video size
Burst shot
Face detection
Metering
ISO
Antishake /video stabilization
Auto night detection
Save as
GPS tag (must be activated when taking pictures for use in Story Album)
Review
Volume key
Timer
White balance
Exposure value
Guidelines
Flash
Voice control
Contextual filename
Save as flipped
Storage
Reset

The Gallery application is used to view photos and videos and is accessed by tapping gallery on the applications screen.

- Launch Gallery to view available folders. Certain application specific folders are created when images are saved, such as the download folder (for pictures saved from emails) and the screenshots folder (for screenshots).
- Pictures are sorted by creation date within the gallery folders. Once a picture has been selected for viewing, you can scroll left or right to view the previous or next picture.
- You can double tap anywhere on a picture to zoom in.
- You can also spread 2 fingers on the picture and pinch to zoom out, spread to zoom in and double tap to return to the original picture size.

Trimming Video

To trim or edit your video, select the video and tap the cutting icon. Place the start bracket where you want the video to start and the end bracket where you want it to end. Save your video.

Editing Images

While looking at a picture, tap Menu to view and use the following editing options:

Favorite
Slideshow
Photo frame
Photo note
Copy to clipboard
Print
Rename
Set as
Buddy photo share
Rotate left
Rotate right
Crop
Detect text
Scan for nearby devices
Details
Settings

To modify the current picture, tap the Edit icon to access the following options:

Rotate
Crop
Color
Effect
Portrait
Sticker
Drawing
Frame

To add the current picture to favorites, tap Menu > favorite.

A picture may be deleted as follows:

- From the folder tap Menu > select item. Tick picture to select and tap the trash bin.

- To delete the current picture tap the trash bin.

- Pictures may be shared from the folder by tapping Menu > select item. Tick picture to select and tap the Send option.
- To send the current picture, tap Send.
- The current picture may be set as wallpaper or assigned to a contact by tapping Menu > set as and choosing the desired option.
- To tag a face in a picture, tap Menu > settings > select Face tag. Tap the face (which should be surrounded by a yellow frame) > add name > choose a contact, or add a new one.
To use tag buddy, tap Menu > settings > Tag buddy > drag the switch to the right.

Story Album

- Use story album to create personalized digital albums, which are organized automatically.
- To access, tap story album on the Applications screen.
- To create a story album automatically, tap create album > by tag information > Choose selection criteria > tap find pictures > give the album a title > choose a theme > tap create album.

- If you want to manually create an album, tap create album > from gallery.
- Your phone will automatically sort pictures taken in a single location into albums based on your current selection criteria and may suggest creating new albums.
- Tap Menu > settings > home city > choose a method to distinguish your location > choose an album type and decide on a minimum number of pictures.

- When you take pictures, which meet your selection criteria your phone will suggest creating an album.

- Tap create album > from suggestions > select album >name album > tap save.

Select your story album to browse it. The first page is your cover picture. Scroll left or right to browse through the pictures contained in the album.
While looking at your pictures, tap Menu to use the following options:

Add content
Remove content
Change theme
Slideshow
Share via
Print
Order photo book
Export
Delete album

The following options are available by tapping pictures in your album:

Add captions
Send pictures
Delete pictures
Apply effects to pictures
Start slideshows
Set picture as album cover picture
Rotate picture clockwise or anticlockwise

Video and YouTube

Tap video on the applications screen to watch video files. Once you have selected the video you want to watch, the following onscreen options become available:

Scan DLNA-enabled devices
Fast forward or rewind by dragging the progress bar
Change screen ratio
Restart current video, skip to previous video, rewind current video
Pause or resume playback
Reduce the size of the video screen
Skip to next video or fast forward current video
Adjust volume

To delete a video, tap Menu > delete > choose videos to be deleted > tap delete.
To share a video, tap Menu > share via > choose videos > tap done > choose a sharing method.

To purchase videos tap download > go to store > choose video.

- To watch videos on the YouTube site tap YouTube on the

Applications screen.

- YouTube is region and service provider dependent.

- Tap the search icon to find content on YouTube > choose a video

from the search results.

Rotate your phone to landscape to watch videos in full screen.

The following options will become available while viewing YouTube content on your phone:

Pause or resume playback.
Fast forward or rewind by dragging the progress bar.
Change display quality.
Rotate the screen to portrait orientation.
Send URL to others.
Search for videos.

Add video to playlist.

- To share a video, tap Share > choose a sharing method.
- To upload a video, tap the upload icon > select your YouTube account > select your video > enter video information > tap the upload icon.

Flipboard

Tap Flipboard on the applications screen to access your personalized magazines. This application is region and service provider specific.

Flipboard is started as follows: flick up on the greeting page > select news topics > tap done.
Choose a cover story or topic > flick through Flipboard pages > choose an article to read.

The following options are available while reading articles:

Go to previous page
Like articles on Facebook
View comments on articles
Share articles with others

Additional Settings

About

This option is used to configure your phone, set application options and add accounts, which can be accessed by tapping Settings on the Applications screen

Connections

Various connection options are available on your phone.

WiFi

Activating WiFi allows you to connect to a WiFi network which gives you access to the Internet or other network devices.

The following options are available by tapping WiFi > Menu:

Advanced
WPS push button
WPS PIN entry
Help

WiFi sleep policy is set by tapping WiFi > Menu > advanced > keep WiFi on during sleep.
When WiFi is turned off, for example when the screen is turned off, your phone will access data networks if set to use them. To avoid additional data charges, set this option to Always.

Tap WiFi > Menu > Advanced > Network notification to detect and display availability of open WiFi networks.

Tap WiFi > WiFi Direct to directly connect two devices using a WiFi network without an access point being necessary.

Bluetooth

Bluetooth is used to transfer data over short distances.
For more Bluetooth options tap Menu. This will give access to:

Visibility timeout
Received files
Help

Data Usage

To keep track of data usage and to set limits use the following options:

- Mobile data
- Set mobile data limit

48

- Data usage cycle

For more options tap Menu
- Data roaming
- Restrict background data
- Auto sync data
- Show WiFi usage
- Mobile hotspots

More Networks

Flight mode:
Disables all wireless functions allowing you to use non-network services only.

Mobile networks:
Mobile data
Data roaming
Access point names
Network mode
Network operators
Tethering and portable hotspot
Portable WiFi hotspot
USB tethering
Bluetooth tethering
Help

VPN
Setting up and connecting to virtual private networks

NFC
NFC – activate to read or write NFC tags which contain data.
Android Beam – activate to send data to NFC enabled devices.
NFC payment – set default payment method

S Beam
Activation of S Beam enables transfer of data such as videos to NFC or WiFi direct enabled devices.

Nearby Devices

File sharing
Shared contents
Allowed devices list
Not allowed devices list
Download to
Upload from other devices

Screen mirroring

Used to share your display with others

Kies via WiFi

Enables connect to Samsung Kies via a WiFi network

My Device

Lock Screen

Locked screen options, which vary according to features selected:

Screen lock
Multiple widgets
Lock screen widgets
Favorite apps or camera
Clock or personal message
Edit personal message
Dual clock
Clock size
Show date
Owner information

Shortcuts
Shortcuts are region and service provider dependent
Unlock effect
Help text
Wake up in lock screen
Set wakeup command

Display

Change display settings:

Wallpaper
-Home screen
-Lock screen
-Home and lock screens

Notification panel
Multi window
Screen mode
Adapt display
Dynamic
Standard
Professional photo
Movie

Brightness
Autorotate screen
Screen timeout
Daydream
Font style
Font size
Touch key light duration
Display battery percentage
Edit after screen capture
Auto adjust screen tone
High touch sensitivity

LED Indicator
Charging
Low battery
Notifications
Voice recording

Sound
Volume
Vibration intensity
Ringtones
Vibrations
Default notification sound
Vibrate when ringing
Dialing keypad tone
Touch sounds
Screen lock sounds
Haptic feedback
Adapt sound

Home Screen Mode

Set home screen mode to basic or easy

Call

Call rejection
Set up call / reject messages
Answering/ending calls:
- The home key answers calls
- Voice control

- The power key ends calls
Turn off screen during calls

Call Alerts

Answer vibration
Call-end vibration
Call connect tone
Minute reminder
Call end tone
Alerts during calls

Call Accessories

The following list provides call accessories for the Samsung Galaxy S4. Most of these items have been listed throughout the text in other categories. This list brings them all together to portray the key elements of the device.

-Automatic answering
-Automatic answering timer
-Outgoing call conditions
-Outgoing call type

Additional settings
-Caller ID
-Call forwarding
-Auto area code
-Call barring
-Call waiting
-Auto redial
-Fixed dialing numbers

Ringtones and keypad tones
-Ringtones
-Vibrations
-Vibrate when ringing
-Keypad tones

Personalize call sound
Noise reduction
Increase volume in pocket
Video call image
Use call fail options
Voicemail service
Voicemail settings
Sound
Vibrate
Accounts
Use Internet calling

Blocking Mode

Choose notifications to block or allow notifications for specified contacts while   blocking mode is active.

Safety Assistance

Enable sending of messages during an emergency. Message is sent when volume up and volume down buttons are pressed and held for 3 seconds.
Edit emergency message
Send emergency pictures
Emergency contacts

Power Saving Mode

Power saving mode activation and settings
-CPU power saving
-Screen power saving
-Turn off haptic feedback
-Learn about power saving mode

Accessory

Adjust accessory settings
-Dock sound
-Audio output mode
-Desk home screen display
-Automatic unlock
-Audio output

Accessibility

The following list describes the many features of the phone in list form. While many of the features have been explained in various sections throughout the guidebook, this list simply puts them all together for you in one location.

Special features for those with certain physical disabilities
- Auto-rotate screen
- Screen timeouts
- Speak passwords
- Answering/ending calls
-The home key answers calls

-Answer calls by tapping
-Voice control
-The power key ends calls
- Show shortcut
- Manage accessibility
- TalkBack
- Font size
- Magnification gestures
- Negative colors
- Color adjustment
- Accessibility shortcut
- Text to speech options
-Preferred TTS engine
-Speech rate
-Listen to an example
- Enhance web accessibility
- Sound balance
- Mono audio
- Turn off all sounds
- Flash notification
- Assistant menu
- Tap and hold delay
- Interaction control

- Language and input
- Language
- Default
- Google voice typing
-Choose input languages
-Block offensive words
-Download offline speech recognition

- Samsung keyboard
-Portrait keyboard types
-Input languages
-Predictive text
-Continuous text
-Cursor control
-Handwriting
-Advanced
-Auto capitalization
-Auto spacing

- -Auto punctuate
- -Character preview
- -Keytap vibration
- -Keytap sound
- -Help
- -Reset settings

- Voice recognizer
- Voice search
  - -Language
  - -Open via the home key
  - -Use location data
  - -Hide offensive words
  - -Help
  - -About
  - -Driving mode
  - -Voice control
  - -Autostart speaker
  - -Show body of message
  - -Wake up command
  - -Wake up in lock screen
  - -Set wake up command
  - -Check missed events
  - -Home address
  - -Log in to Facebook
  - -Log in to twitter
- Google voice recognition used the following:
  - -Language
  - -Speech output
  - -Block offensive words
  - -Download offline speech recognition

- Text to speech options
  - -Preferred TTS engine
  - -Speech rate
  - -Listen to an example
- Pointer speed
  - -Motions and gestures
- Air gesture
  - -Learn about sensor and icon
  - -Quick glance
  - -Air jump

-Air browse
-Air move
-Air call-accept

- Motion
  -Direct call
  -Smart alert
  -Zoom
  -Browse an image
  -Mute/pause
- Palm motion
  -Capture screen
  -Mute/pause
- Gyroscope calibration
  -Smart screen
  -Smart stay
  -Smart rotation
  -Smart pause
  -Smart scroll
    -Scroll by
    -Speed
    -Visual feedback display
    -Air view
-Information preview
-Progress preview
-Speed dial preview
-Webpage magnifier
-Sound and haptic feedback

Voice control
-Adjust voice command options

Multiple Accounts

The following sections describe settings that include Add Account, Cloud, and Backup, or Reset. These functions are valuable for those who plan to share a phone, use the Cloud system or who may have to reset a phone for any reason.

Add Account—For additional email or SNS accounts

Cloud—Change settings for Samsung account or Dropbox storage

Backup and Reset:

- Backup my data
- Backup account
- Automatic restore
- Factory data reset

Using the Web

Internet

Tap Internet on the applications screen to browse the Internet

To view web pages:

- Tap address field > enter web address > tap go

- Tap Menu to share, save or print web content

- Tap address field > search engine icon to change the search

engine

Opening a new page
Tap Menu > new window

Bookmarks
Tap Menu > add bookmark to save the current page

History
Tap Menu > History to view history
Tap Menu > clear history to clear history

Links
Tap and hold a link to open in new page, save or copy
Saved links are accessible via download

Sharing web pages
Tap Menu > Share

Dropbox

Dropbox is used for saving and sharing content with others via Dropbox cloud storage

- Tap Dropbox on the applications screen to access
- Tap start to activate Dropbox for first time usage
- Photos and videos taken with the phone's camera are automatically uploaded to Dropbox once it has been activated

Cloud

This feature enables you to synchronize files or back up data and settings using Dropbox or your Samsung account.

- Activate by tapping settings > accounts > cloud on the applications screen.
- Tap sync settings to synchronize data with your Samsung account.
- To back up or restore data using your Samsung account, tap backup.
- To synchronize using Dropbox, tap link Dropbox account > enter Dropbox account > follow onscreen instructions.
- Automatic synchronization is enabled by tapping allow after signing in.

S Voice

Tap S Voice on the applications screen or press home twice.

Once active, you can use voice commands to dial numbers, send messages, etc.

Some spoken commands:

- Open music

- Launch calculator

- Call Greg mobile

- Dial Gary work

- Check schedule

For better voice recognition speak clearly in a quiet place, avoiding slang and offensive language. Avoid dialectal accents.

Driving Mode

When driving mode is active, the phone will read some content out loud for incoming calls, messages and notifications.

- Say "Driving mode on" or tap Menu > set driving mode on to activate.
- Driving mode can be set up to activate automatically in specified locations by tapping Menu > settings > driving mode > my places for driving mode > set my place.

My Files

Tap my files on the applications screen to activate my files, which allows access to various types of files stored on the phone, such as video, pictures, and more.
Select a folder for opening. To return to previous folder, tap the previous folder icon. To return to root directory, tap the home icon.

Tap Menu in a folder to access the following options:

- Select all

- Create folder

- Search

- View by

- Sort by

- Settings

Tap Menu > add shortcut > name your shortcut > select folder > tap set here to add a shortcut to the root directory

Downloads

Tap downloads in the applications screen to see which files have been downloaded through applications.

Additional options:

- Sort by size
- Sort by date
- File selection opens files with the appropriate application

Optical reader

On the applications screen tap optical reader to scan or extract text or data from   various sources.

To scan text, aim the pointer at an image, document or QR code.
- Text – see meanings of extracted words.
- Business cards – make calls from scanned contact data
- QR codes – view data for QR codes

Maps

Activate by tapping Maps on the applications screen, searching for locations. Tap the search icon > type in an address > tap the search icon again > select the desired location to view information.

Once you have found the desired location, tap Menu for the following options:

Clear map
Make available offline
Directions
Layers
Settings
Help

To find directions for a location, tap the Directions icon> tap the Direction icon > select an option for start and end location:

My current location
Contacts
Point on map
My places

Choose a travel method and tap GET DIRECTIONS > choose a route > tap MAP VIEW.

Local

Tap local on the applications screen to search for nearby places of interest.
Select a place category and choose one of the following:

- Map
- Directions
- Call

Tap Menu > add a search on the category list > type in a search keyword to add a place category.

Navigation

This application allows you to search for a route to a destination and is activated by tapping navigation in the applications screen.

Destinations may be specified as follows:

- Speak the address

- Type in the address

- Select from contacts

- Select from starred places

Troubleshooting Problems

Issue	Issue key words	Action
Your phone prompts you to enter one of the following codes	Password	If the lock feature is enabled, you must enter a password
	PIN	Enter PIN
	PUK	SIM or USIM is blocked due to incorrect PIN attempts – enter PUK supplied by service provider
	PIN2	Enter PIN2 – in need contact service provider
Network or service error message	Weak signal	Move to area with stronger signal
	Subscription required	Contact your service provider
Touch screen slow or improper response		Remove any protective covers
		Ensure hands are clean and dry
		Restart device
		Confirm whether you have the latest software version on your phone
		In cases where the screen is scratched/damage refer to local Samsung dealer
Device freezes/fatal errors		Close programs
		Reset device
		Hold power button for more than 7 seconds to reboot

		On applications screen tap settings > accounts > backup and reset > factory data reset > reset device > erase everything
Dropped calls	Poor signal	Move to find stronger signal
Outgoing calls not connecting		Press dial key
		Confirm that correct cellular network is active
		Check call barring settings
Incoming calls not connecting		Check whether phone is switched on
		Confirm that correct cellular network is active
		Check call barring settings
Others cannot hear you speaking		Make sure the microphone is not covered
		Hold microphone close to your mouth
		If headset is in use make sure that it is properly connected
Poor audio quality		Make sure the antenna is not covered
	Poor signal	Move to find stronger signal
Calls dialed from contacts not connecting		Confirm number
		Reenter and save number
		Check call barring settings
Empty battery icon accompanied by beeping		Charge or replace battery

Device turns off or battery does not charge properly		Clean gold-colored battery terminals with soft, clean cloth
		Safely dispose of old battery and replace with a new battery
Device is heating up		This is normal
Error messages when camera is launched		Charge or replace battery
		Free memory by deleting or transferring files
		Restart device
		Contact Samsung service center
Error messages when music files are open		Free memory by deleting or transferring files
		If file is DRM protected, make sure you have the correct license
		Ensure that files are in a supported format
Bluetooth devices not being found		Activate Bluetooth
		Activate Bluetooth on other device
		Make sure devices are less than 10m apart
		If all else fails, contact Samsung service center
Unable to connect to computer		Ensure that you are using a compatible USB cable
		Check the drivers on the computer
		Make sure that computer software is up to date

		Check that windows media player is at least version 10 or that Kies is at least version 2.0
The device case appears to be cracking		This is normal